THE BUTTERFLY'S
cage

Shahnaz Khari

THE BUTTERFLY'S
cage

Edited by Chris Newton

MEMOIRS
Cirencester

Published by Memoirs

MEMOIRS

Memoirs Books

25 Market Place, Cirencester, Gloucestershire, GL7 2NX
info@memoirsbooks.co.uk www.memoirsbooks.co.uk

Copyright ©Shahnaz Khari, June 2011
First published in England, June 2011
Book jacket design Ray Lipscombe

ISBN 978-1-908223-10-4

Printed in England

Contents

Acknowledgements

I would like to thank my niece Sami for helping me with this book, my younger brother Bilal, who was there for my daughter when I could not be, and Chris and Tony at Memoirs Books for their help in editing and publishing my story.

With love to my daughter, and may God always be with her.

Shahnaz

June 2011

CHAPTER 1

It was a beautiful day and the flowers in the garden were looking astonishing. I was in my dream world as usual, gazing out of the window, when I heard my mother's voice.

"Shahnaz!" she called. "What are you doing up there?"

"Nothing, Mum" I shouted. "I'm coming."

I ran down the stairs and into the kitchen, where my two sisters were chatting and doing the cooking. I knew what my mother wanted me for. I stood at the sink and started to wash the dishes.

"You'd better wash them properly," yelled my older sister Sheana. I carried on washing and they carried on talking. I wasn't included in the conversation. I just went back to my dreaming as I washed up.

My sisters and mother were always talked about their weddings. Sheana and Rehanna were in their teens and I was 12, so they were not so much older than me. But their lives were changing. Soon they would be getting married back home in Pakistan. They would go shopping with my mother, then run up to their rooms and look through all the things they had bought.

I would walk up the stairs quietly and slowly, step by step towards the excited voices. Then I would try to peep into the room. Sometimes my mother would call me inside in a friendly voice. Other times I would get shouted at and kicked out of the room, and my sisters would tell me I was too young to be in the same room as them. When that happened I would sit with my young brother Zaid. I never understood why I was too young to sit with my sisters and had to be sent to my brother's room. Surely I was old enough to look at their beautiful dresses, jewellery and makeup? I didn't fit in with Zaid, who just liked playing with his toy cars and aeroplanes.

One night I was feeling frightened, so I knocked on my sisters' bedroom door. I could hear them talking and giggling inside. They asked me what I wanted, but before I could even answer I was told to buzz off. I sat outside the door. At least I felt safe there, and I could hear their voices, which gave me a little strength.

I looked at my mother's bedroom door, which was firmly shut. I did not dare to knock on that door. My father was a businessman who worked very hard, and he needed all the sleep he could get.

I got up and tiptoed to Zaid's room. I went in and slowly crawled into his bed. I tried to go to sleep on the other side of the bed, but he woke up and asked what I was doing. I told him I was scared, so he let me stay.

That summer my parents flew to Pakistan with my sisters and left me in the house with my grandmother and my brothers. I had to leave school to stay at home looking after my brothers. I also had to clean the house, and it was a very big house. That was a new experience for me, as I never had to do all the housework and get my brothers ready for school. Sometimes I would forget to put the washing on in time, so my brothers had to wear socks that didn't match. My grandmother helped me to learn to cook and clean. But I still wanted to go to school and learn like all the other children who were my age.

Life was even worse when my father returned from Pakistan. When he left to go to work he would tell me to clean the house, and then when he returned he would find me asleep after all the work I had had to do. I remember him shouting at me at six one morning to get cleaning. My older brother Shan woke up at the sound of his father shouting. He was in tears. I just walked down and started to do the vacuuming without having any breakfast. Then I had to serve breakfast to the rest of the family, as my brothers had to go school and my father had to go to work.

Once everyone had left, I would do the cleaning and cooking and look after all the jobs a housewife does. I would dream about getting married, because that seemed to be the only way for me to get out of the life of drudgery I was having to lead.

My mother was away in Pakistan for six months. When she came back she took over everything, with me helping. She was nice to me, but she didn't really understand what I was going through. She would just say, "You know your father." I asked her if I could go back to school and catch up with my studies, but once father had made a decision, nothing could be done about it. I never went back to school.

I didn't make any friends at home as I was never allowed out except with mother, and only when she went shopping on a Saturday.

That is how my life was until I was 18 years old. Then everything changed. One day my father told me he had accepted a proposal of marriage on my behalf.

He was at least kind enough to ask me if I was happy about it. I didn't mind that a husband had been chosen for me, I was just happy with the thought of escaping from the life I was living. I had known the man, whose name was Umar, since childhood, and I was told he really wanted to marry me and was in love with me. Hearing those words at 18 when you've led such a sheltered life, as I had, who wouldn't want to say yes? Umar was a tall and handsome man, and his father was known for his honour and wealth. I was so lucky!

In any case, saying no to my father was out of the question. My parents had a way of asking questions which gave me only one choice of answer. My mother was a religious woman. She knew how to stand on a prayer mat and how to keep God happy. I was happy and excited about it. I kept saying to myself "Yes! At last I will live my life fully and in peace".

Everyone else in my family had been able to finish their schooling. They hadn't had to stay at home looking after their siblings from the age of 12. So the rest of the people out there must be good people. The family I was going to be married into were said to be a nice family, open-minded.

One morning my mother woke me up and told me to get ready, because it was time to do the wedding shopping. Wedding shopping – just as my sisters had done! I began to feel like a free woman.

Even my father had changed towards me. He was more relaxed and calm. I think he had realized I was going to leave the house soon, and I thought he wanted me to be happy. Maybe he felt at peace knowing that all three of his daughters would soon be married and not his responsibility anymore.

My big day was set, and I stayed awake all night thinking about what lay in store for me. I would be starting a new life with different people, not like my father who was so strict. Nice people, a loving husband… it was all so wonderful! Bells rang in my head and I could hear birds singing. I imagined I could already hear the wedding guests going up and down the stairs. I heard Zaid, who couldn't wait to put his three-piece suit on. "NOW mother, can I put it on?" he would shout and I heard my mother saying "No not yet Zaid, you will make it dirty." I laughed about it all, sitting alone in my room and dreaming.

I stayed in my room for nearly a week before the wedding because I had been told not to work in the house for a change, just to relax. You can imagine what I had been doing - taking out all my dresses and things for the wedding and checking them, every couple of hours. Soon my cousins would come and I would be so glad to show them what my parents had brought for me as gifts. My father was a rich man, so I had been given everything I liked, everything I wanted. I had gold jewellery, nice bedroom furniture, expensive clothes, fashionable shoes and bags. I would tell my mother what I wanted and she would pass it on to him. I couldn't help giggling at my own happiness.

My sisters were there helping with the preparations. They had their own lives now that they were married. They both had children and were happy and fulfilled.

My wedding day went as joyfully as I had hoped. Umar told me how beautiful I looked and how happy he was to have me as his wife. As the day went on people kept coming up to greet us.

"It's like a doll getting married" one of my uncles said. He smiled and put his hands on my head and told me I was still a child for him and always would be. We went through the Asian ceremony and it all went very well.

When it was time to leave my parents' house my heart was thumping and I was shaking. I was going out into a different world. It would be a better life - no more shouting, no more restrictions. And yet - I was leaving my family home! All my memories were in that house.

My family all said goodbye to me in turn. I had a very big family, so it took a long time. As I was escorted to the car my father came to say goodbye. I started to shake. I was going to miss him and I knew he would miss me, because I was his favourite. All these years I had done as he had told me.

He came close and hugged me, and we were both in tears. Was that really my father, crying? He didn't want to let me go, but my brothers and uncles drew him away. He cried, and even told me was sorry. I cried more than he did - he was my father. My brothers just stood there watching me leave. I could tell by their expressions that they were happy for me and were glad I was to be free.

When we reached my new in-laws' house they greeted me with happiness and they all seemed over the moon. They took me to my bedroom, where I sat on the bed with my heavy dress and beautiful gold jewellery. The women of the family came one by one to admire me and praise me and tell me how beautiful I looked. My new husband kept coming into the room and then going back out again, waiting for all the visitors to go.

At one point I was left alone in the room, and as I sat there I heard a sudden commotion downstairs. My sister Sheana was there and so was her husband, so I thought I would wait for them to come up and tell me what the noise was.

Then I heard a loud shout – it sounded like my uncle's voice. For a few seconds I froze in shock. What could he be doing here?

I got up and slowly walked out of the room – it was difficult to move in that heavy wedding dress. I leaned over to look downstairs.

I could not believe what I saw. The voice was not my uncle's. It was my husband's. He was shouting and screaming at a young woman who had come to the house. She was very attractive, but I could see that she was drunk. With her was a white girl, who was screaming in support of her friend.

"He is the father of my child!" the first woman kept screaming, pointing to Umar. "She is lying!" he shouted back. The passage was crowded with relatives. The men were trying to calm her down, but she would not. In the end they pushed her out of the house and slammed the door.

I rushed back upstairs to my room. Sheana came in, looking as if she had been crying. She didn't say anything about what had happened. She just said she was crying because she was going to miss me. Then she left the room, saying she was in a hurry. I knew there was nothing she could do.

Then Umar came into the room and sat beside me. He looked confused. I asked him what had happened, and he said one of his aunts had fallen down the stairs and hurt herself. I tried to pretend I believed him. I didn't want to believe what I had seen and heard from the stairs, and I felt too weak to fight or argue. I thought, what a good actor I have married!

We talked for a while, and he told me that sometimes he said things he didn't mean because of some medicine he was taking which caused drowsiness. I felt lost and confused. Perhaps what had happened was somehow normal. In any case, whatever the truth of it, my father was too strict to take me back, even if I wanted to go back. I was going to have to try and have a happy life with this man – this man who was telling me things that didn't make sense.

CHAPTER 2

I had no idea of the horror my married life would turn out to be. I dreaded the nights and I dreaded the days. My new husband was a monster. I was forced to do things I hated. He would make me do things which were horrible and painful, and if I begged and cried to him to stop he would laugh. I would be confused and ask him what he was doing to me and he would tell me I was not woman enough.

At times I would lie that I was desperate to use the toilet and would stay there for a while and pray that he would fall asleep. I sat alone and cried for hours, but no-one seemed to notice my tears.

One day I went to see my parents. The day went happily and I joked and bantered with my brothers and showed off my new clothes. No-one asked me about what had happened on the wedding day. Perhaps they had not been told, or perhaps everyone knew but was trying to keep it from me. I had no way of knowing.

When it was time for my parents to drop me off, I felt as if a fishbone was stuck in my throat. I was sick and scared. I didn't want to go back to Umar, but I had no choice. Who would listen to me if I told them what had happened, what was still happening? And I could not forget what my father was like. He might refuse to talk to me.

My mother-in-law was like my own mother, a lady with rules

and regulations. She was nice to me as I was nice to her, she would smile as I would smile. But I knew that if I had told her any of what had happened she would say, how dare you say that! She was a very strict lady. Once she said to me "Your mother hasn't taught you anything!"

But it was easy for me to keep quiet. I was used to listening to my elders and obeying everything they said, even if it was wrong. My mother always said, "Respect your elders and say yes to whatever they say", even if they told you to jump off a cliff! I had learned the lesson well.

When I entered the house my mother-in-law and father-in-law gave me a warm welcome and asked me if I had enjoyed my day. I began to relax a little. I told them I couldn't wait to come back. "That's nice to hear," said my father in law. "This is your house and you will be looking after it." Yes, I thought, I know how to look after a house – a bigger one than this, and all on my own.

I walked into my bedroom, where Umar was watching TV. He gave me a friendly welcome and cuddled me as if he didn't want to let me go. I was surprised at that, but I took it as a gift sent by God, and wrapped the moment in my heart.

I put my stuff away and we sat down and chatted together. I was happy and excited. He really had missed me, and maybe he had realised what I was to him. I didn't doubt him for once. Surely he was not acting now. Perhaps my mother was right when she had said that if you keep calm and keep trying you will get what you want in life.

Then Umar looked at me. "I need to talk to you," he said. "I want you to listen carefully, as I have something to tell you." I smiled and nodded my head.

"I was addicted to heroin and cocaine," he said. I must have looked confused. What were heroin and cocaine? But I knew "addiction" was not a good word. "Drugs" he said.

I froze. I couldn't move an inch.

"But it's sorted" he said. "I had some treatment while you were at your parents" house." One day of treatment for drug addiction? That didn't sound right.

"I had to pay a lot of money for the treatment. I really needed it. I wanted to start a fresh life." I smiled again and gave him a cuddle.

"It's ok, at least you're all fine now" I said.

"But that's not the point" he said

"Why?"

"I took your gold," he said

"My gold? What do you mean?"

"The gold your mother had given you. I had to sell the bracelet and some other jewellery to get the money for treatment."

I wanted to scream and cry out loud. The gold had been a wedding gift from my parents. I had already given the money I had been given at my wedding to his family, but this was stealing. I was terribly hurt, but I managed to keep my emotions under control.

"OK" I said. "It's OK now that you're all over the drugs."

I didn't sleep that night. I had never really slept since I had been married to this man.

Of course, he wasn't over his addiction at all. It wasn't long before he started to bring drugs into our room. I was now three months pregnant. My mother-in-law asked me if my mother or sisters had told me about the pill – but of course they hadn't. All I knew was how to clean the house and how to keep my mouth shut. I felt a little betrayed by my family for pushing me into this new life without any guidance other than "Be nice to your in-laws, they are like your parents", "Obey your husband, he is like God, you never say no" (specially if he is holding a sharp knife and threatening to slice your throat with it). "Do not steal, do not take anything from the house" and so on.

At night I was treated like a dog. If I complained he would beat me up, saying I was not woman enough. When I cried he would hit me more. I just had to let him do what he wanted and then turn away and cover my mouth as I wept. If I had some money he would take it from me and use it on drugs, so I never had money to spend on myself. The only peace I would get was when I spent time with my mother or my brothers. I always dreaded coming back home to him.

The time came when my father-in-law left to go to Pakistan. After he left things got even worse. When he became seriously ill my mother-in-law went to join him, leaving me alone with my drug-addict husband and my younger brother-in-law and sister-in-law. They were very nice to me, but they were too young to know what was happening in the house, let alone to do anything to help me. I would take them to school, which was half a mile down the road, and cook and clean. I also started to do some work from home, just to get some money in as my mother-in-law had requested.

God had now given me the best gift I could possibly wish for, a lovely daughter, whom I called Henna. She was so beautiful. My family supported me and bought me baby things. My brothers and sisters also gave me gifts, but Umar was too busy with his own world and too affected by his drug-taking to provide anything. He even took Henna's child benefit money every week and spent it on himself. I stopped working at home, not because I had a baby to look after but because he would take the money from my boss and say I had asked for it.

At one point he woke me up in the middle of the night because he wanted something to eat. I was fast asleep and didn't realize what was happening until he pressed his lighted cigarette on to my arm. I screamed, but he just giggled as if it was funny. Sixteen years later I still have the burn mark.

Then he started to send me out to beg for money from his friends. He would get angry if I said no, so I would come back and tell him that the people weren't home and that the door had been opened by some men who didn't seem respectable, and he shouldn't send me there again. Then he would start to swear and hit me. Sometimes I would take the children out until he had left.

One morning when I went to drop the children off to school a family friend asked me if I was OK. She said my husband had come round asking for money because I was ill. He had been round the previous week as well, saying I needed money for milk for the baby.

I was very shocked. I told the woman not to give him money any more as I would never ask for it. I said I would pay back the money she had given him.

My father-in-law died while he and my mother-in-law were still in Pakistan. When she came back after the funeral, Umar had sold nearly everything in the house. All that was left was a few pieces of furniture. He sold my jewellery, even my hairdryer and my daughter's pushchair. He also started to bring men back to the house and they would take drugs together. It was getting very scary for me as the men used the house however they wanted. I would put the children to sleep and wait in my room for the men to go.

It got so bad that Umar would tell me to go and ask people for money, and say that if I didn't get it he would set the house on fire.

When I tried asking someone older to talk to him he would threaten to kill himself. He would go out in the night and steal stereos from cars and sell them the next morning. One day he came home with a woman's credit cards. He had obviously mugged someone and stolen their bag. The police would knock on the door and he would escape through a window. No-one could stop him.

In the end I phoned Zaid and told him he had to come and take me away. Everyone by now had begun to realise what I was going through. I told my husband he needed help, but I could not be there for him. I had to look after my child.

When Zaid arrived he helped me to collect my husband's brothers and sisters and our belongings and we drove away. Umar didn't say much - he just watched me leave. He didn't try to stop me.

I dropped the children at my sister-in-law's house and made

my way back to my parents' house. My parents had changed towards me at last. They understood what I had been through.

I walked through the door and threw my arms around my mother. I cried and cried to get all the pain out of my system. My father hugged me too. "Everything will be fine now," he said. "You're in a safe place." Henna was only nine months old, so she would not remember what had happened.

I went to the bedroom where I had once sat alone and cried to myself. I felt a little uncomfortable, but it was much better than the life I had left behind. I could breathe more easily, begin to relax.

I stayed with my parents for the next three years. My father did not like me leaving the house, because he said I would be alone. I did have some ups and downs with my parents. They were still strict and did not want me to study, because they said there was no point. I looked after them and they looked after me. By now Shan was also married and living there and we all got on well.

Sometimes Umar came with his mother to take Henna. They would pick her up in the morning and drop her off in the evening. He tried to persuade me to make a new start with him as he said he had changed, but I did not believe him. My mother-in-law pleased for me to take him back and my father sent me back to him again. But this time it was even worse. He had syringes lying around in the room for drugs. He had stolen passports and credit cards. Later I found out he was dealing with drugs.

My mother-in-law had changed towards me and started to see

me as a bad girl. If I made a phone call to my parents she would make me sit with all her children and tell them what I had said to my mother. She would make me walk miles to the clinic to get powdered milk for my daughter, on a hot summer day. Sometimes I had hardly any money and I would search the pavement hoping to find a few pence for a drink, as it was so hot.

Then one day she threw me and my daughter out of the house, just because I spoke up and told her that she should look at what her son was doing before putting so much pressure on me. Umar tried to come with me, but I would not let him. My father accepted that I couldn't handle all this and I went back to live with my parents. Two and a half years later, we were divorced.

One day out of the blue, my family decided we were going to Pakistan. I was happy and excited about taking my baby there, and I needed the break. We started to prepare for the holiday, and I bought a lot of things for myself and my daughter. I felt I was over all the bad things that had happened to me.

My brothers were all with us. Zaid was 19 years old now and very good-looking, with greenish eyes. The girls adored him, and he was a little too proud of it. Everyone was excited and talking loudly. My mother hissed at us to keep the noise down. "What will these people say, we have respect here, keep your voices down!" she said.

We landed in Pakistan and collected our luggage. Some family friends had come to meet us and we all greeted each other. It was hot and dusty and there were many people walking around. There were many beggars. I liked giving to beggars because I always thought they needed money more than me. My daughter was now three years old and very cute and pretty (she still is). She chatted and asked me lots of questions.

Our house was huge, a real mansion. My father had built it for his family when I was small. It was beautiful. I had been there before, but it always seemed as if I was seeing it for the first time. Henna was impressed. "Wow Mummy, this is nice!" she said.

We chose our rooms and started to unpack.

We had a lovely time in Pakistan. We met many nice people and visited lots of places of interest. I was only allowed to go out with my brothers and had to wear a big shawl – that's how it is in Pakistan. My brothers were great fun and my daughter loved them – she listened to them much more than she listened to me.

When my father came and joined us, things changed a little. We went out less and the rules were stricter - we were not allowed to stand at the balcony and look at the crowds! Otherwise everything was fine. More people visited us, and many of them wanted to see me and present proposals of marriage! Mothers would come to visit, and send their sons to meet me. They would send presents for my mum. This is the way things are done in Pakistan.

One morning I woke up and walked out across the lawn to enjoy the morning sunshine. It was a glorious, hot day and the flowers were all looking beautiful. I felt happier than ever.

As I rounded the corner of the house I saw my parents sitting on the lawn having tea. They did not notice me approaching.

"I want her to get married to someone here" I heard my father say. They were talking about me! I stood there wondering whether to listen or walk away. But it was my life they were talking about.

"You think before you decide, she is our daughter and she has a daughter of her own" said my mother. "I have a few boys in mind and I'll ask her."

I walked slowly backwards, went back up to my room and curled up in bed. It took a long time for the tears to stop. I kept wondering who my father considered the right man for me.

The rest of the day I stayed quiet. I wanted my mother to tell me herself what was going on, but she said nothing. I made an effort to get her to talk. "Mum, what was Dad saying to you this morning?" I asked her. She was cutting bhindi bhaji, ladies' fingers. She looked up at me. "He was just saying that we need to think about your future," she said. "You're still young."

"Do I have to get married again? Can't I just stay the way I am and wait for the right person to come into my life?"

"Right person? What are you talking about! Your dad is going to find you a suitable person here in Pakistan. We can't keep coming back here, so we need to get it over and done with while we're here."

There was silence for a while. At last she said, "You'll have a choice".

"How is that a choice? I don't want to get married to anyone!" I said. But I knew my father's decision would be final. It all seemed so unfair. His nieces had not been forced to get married, so why me?

"Your father wants you to get married and so do I, and don't forget he has done a lot for you" she said. "He has a good name and respect. We're not going to just throw you into it. We will take time looking for someone."

I wanted to say "Have you forgotten what I have done for you?" but I couldn't speak up. Even though I was a mother myself now, I was still scared of my father. I would shake when he addressed me. There was no way I was going to fight with him. His rules had to be obeyed.

CHAPTER 3

The proposals came along and my father rejected them all. There was one man he quite liked, and he and his family started coming every day to see us. One of the sons was married to my aunt and they were related to my father and mother, so my father felt this family was the right one.

The aunt had two unmarried sons. One was young and had had little education, but the other was older and highly qualified. He was very nice and intelligent. When father was not around he would come and sit for hours and chat, and we seemed to get on, so I felt there was no problem with me getting married to him, and told my mother.

She passed the message to my father, but he said I was choosing the wrong son. They had suggested the younger one, Wasim, should be my husband. But I was not prepared to get married to someone I had never met and only seen once very briefly. I tried to put my foot down.

Of course, my father got angry with me. "They are brothers! They are the same!" he said. For a long time after that we did not speak to each other. Dad kept looking at me as if he had caught me sleeping with someone.

In the end I agreed to marry the younger son. My parents were relieved. I had made the right choice, they said. Wasim was only 20 years old and was still at college.

One day I was sitting alone on the lawn when my sister

Rehanna came out and sat next to me. "My husband says you are standing near a river, and shall we push you?" This was her way of asking me if it was a yes or no to whether they were to proceed with the engagement ceremony of my father giving my hand to his parents. They knew it was not right, but my father would not listen. Sheana phoned my father from England and told him that the boy was not the right person for me. My uncle did the same. But my father just shouted at them. "I have given my word!" he said.

My new husband looked very young, and he seemed to me to talk like a child. But the marriage date was only a few months away. My brothers were confused about it all. My little daughter was too young to understand what her mother was being put through. At least, I thought, arranged marriages sometimes work well. Not everyone was like my first husband.

Slowly I came round to the idea of getting married to Wasim. I talked to him over the phone and he seemed OK. He told me he had fallen in love with me when he had seen me in a family movie, and was happy to keep my daughter as his own, which was nice of him to say. His parents and sisters were very nice, highly educated people.

I would go shopping every day with my family. I bought loads of stuff and my father paid for more gold jewellery. I was given everything I wanted.

My daughter was excited and happy with her new dresses. She did not understand what was going on, but she gets excited about it and shows all her stuff to visitors. "Mummy getting married" she would say.

21

The night before the wedding I was awake all night thinking about what was going to happen. I was scared and nervous because I had had such a bad experience before.

In the morning Shan got me ready. She was quiet, and seemed a little down. I told her not to worry. I was ready to walk down the stairs where Wasim was waiting when I looked and peeped out. He looked like a little boy sitting there, looking very nervous. Am I really doing this, I asked myself? If only I could have married someone a little older and more mature.

The day went past happily enough for everyone, and when it was time to leave my family met me. My mother cuddled me and cried, my father hugged and kissed me on my forehead. I cried and wanted to scream - why are you lot doing this to me? I had a bad feeling about it, but of course it was too late.

I was greeted very warmly by everyone in my in-laws' house. There were women waiting to see the bride. They made me sit on a chair and filmed me for a movie. The women were all praising me and saying how pretty I was, but I felt like saying, I am hurt and in pain. I am trying to look happy but I'm not happy, not happy at all.

At last my sister-in-law took me up to my bedroom. I sat down and Wasim walked in. He sat on the corner of the bed looking nervous. He didn't seem to be able to speak properly. His voice kept getting stuck in his throat. Then he spoke at last.

"I'm sorry, my friends gave me a tablet and I might say things I don't mean," he said, giggling.

A tablet - he was on drugs? I screamed inside my head. My past with my first husband came right back to me. I couldn't believe this was happening again.

That night I prayed in silence. "Oh God, please do not do this to me, not now, what have I done wrong to be punished like this!"

In the morning I was awoken by the sound of the overnight guests. Wasim was getting ready to go out and sit with the visitors. They had invited nearly the whole town to the house and I had to get dressed in my beautiful new pink and green dress and matching jewellery. When I was ready they made me come out and sit on a chair with all these people looking at me. Some tried talking to me and some just sat and stared. I kept looking at the time, as I was waiting for my daughter and my family to arrive.

At the meal I sat and talked to Wasim. I spoke Urdu and Punjabi, as he didn't speak much English. His brothers joined us and we all joked and bantered with each other. I knew the family from before.

When my parents arrived at eight o'clock that evening I was very disappointed to see that my daughter was not with them. I was annoyed with my mother for not bringing her, but she told me Henna had wanted to come with her cousins and my sister's family, who would be arriving the next day, when we had yet another family get-together planned.

The next morning I wore a richly-embroidered blue and gold dress, which I had bought with my father and mother. When he saw how much I liked it, my father had bought it without even asking the price.

"You are looking even more beautiful today," said my mother when she saw me, and she kissed me on my forehead. I said that was because I had done my make-up myself. The first two days I had been plastered with make-up like a clay model. My eye was on the main door, because I was waiting for my sister to arrive with my daughter. I was missing her.

Finally at a quarter to two Rehanna arrived. Her family were with her, but there was no sign of Henna. No-one seemed to be able to tell me where she was. I was very puzzled and a little annoyed.

Finally a family friend told me what had happened. "She is staying with your friend," she said. "Your mother-in-law asked your mother not to bring her until at least a week after the wedding."

I was horrified. "Why?" I asked her. I didn't care who was listening. But I didn't want to create a scene until I understood what had happened.

I asked my mother where Henna was. She looked at me as if I had asked the wrong question. "She is at home with your aunt and some babysitters," she said. "Don't worry, she's ok."

She told me my mother-in-law hadn't wanted my daughter clinging on to me while I was posing as the newly-wed bride in front of all those people. I was stunned that she had hidden this from me.

"She's my daughter!" I shouted. "She comes first! Who the hell are they to tell me when I can have her with me!"

My mother told me to calm down. It wasn't such a big deal, she said. I had a new life to think about now. But I didn't understand how she could talk like that. I just wanted to rip off my wedding dress. I felt it was burning me.

I didn't sleep at all that night. I lay there beside my husband, crying secretly. I hated him too now, because I knew he was part of this. Shame on these people, I thought. She is only a little girl and she has never been away from me. My parents must have known what was going on, but they didn't have the guts to tell me.

At last the wedding festivities and socialising were all over and I was able to phone Henna. She sounded happy and excited, because my brother had taken her out and had bought lots of stuff for her. It was a relief to know she was OK.

Then, as I was about to go into the shower, I heard my brothers-in-law talking in the hall. Wasim had left to see some friends. I could hear their conversation clearly. They were having some sort of argument.

"He wasn't a baby, he knew what he was doing" said the older brother. He sounded angry.

"But if the word had come out it would have brought shame on the family" relied his brother.

"He got a girl pregnant in this house, and where were you" said the first one. "I feel like beating him up."

"Just leave it. He is married, everything is sorted."

I walked to my bed and sat there quietly for an hour. I did not want to believe what I had heard. But I didn't cry. I felt as if I had cried all my tears already.

Now I knew there was something the family was hiding from me. I realized that my older brother-in-law never seemed to speak to my husband, who would disappear whenever he was around. I made my mind up to find out what had happened.

Once I had had my breakfast, I went looking for my brother-in-law. I felt we were good friends, but I knew he had hidden the truth. I found him reading a newspaper in the sitting room.

"I heard you and your brother talking about my husband," I said. "I want to know the truth."

His face went pale. "We were talking about someone else," he said, looking away. He was lying, of course. "I heard everything," I said. "I want to know the truth." But he would not talk.

It was all beginning to make sense. This was the reason they had insisted on me marrying their younger son, even though in Pakistani families sons are usually married off in order of their age.

I think my brother-in-law must have told the rest of the family about our conversation, because they all suddenly became too busy to talk to me.

I went up to Wasim. I told him I knew everything, and someone had told me what he had done. At first he just giggled and walked away, but I followed him. I told him it was in the past and it was of no concern to me, but that I was curious and wanted to know if it was all true.

"Yes, it is true" he said, still smiling. I felt like digging a big hole and throwing him in it.

He told me the whole story. It had happened only a few months before. A girl had been living in their house who was married but was waiting for her visa. While she was there Wasim had got her pregnant, and as she was married and it would have been a big shame on the family, they had had the child aborted. She had been taken away by her relatives.

I asked him why he hadn't married her. "She was a whore, she was no good. She was the one who kept coming on to me all the time." You men! I thought. That poor girl.

Of course, I just had to ignore what I knew and carry on with my marriage. This was my second wedding, so my family would say I was in the wrong. A divorcee could not criticise her husband's behaviour, because it would be thought that she was lucky to find another man who would take her.

I didn't make a big fuss about it. I just told Wasim he had done wrong.

The next day they agreed to let me pick up my daughter. It was wonderful to see my sweet and lovely Henna. When she saw me she ran as fast as she could to greet me. I kissed and cuddled her. I had missed her so much.

"Mummy, where were you?" she said. I wanted to say - in a new hell, my little one!

My parents and brothers were pleased to see me too, and we spent the day chatting and laughing.

In the afternoon I went to see my aunt and her daughter who also had come from England. They knew my in-laws and my new husband well. It was a tidy house with a pleasant atmosphere. My uncle, my father's younger brother, was much more open-minded than my father and his daughter had more freedom.

It was all fine until my aunt asked Wasim how old he was. He giggled and didn't reply. "He's 21" I said. They laughed as if I had told a joke, but I couldn't see what was so funny. Wasim tried to change the subject, but my aunt wouldn't let him.

"You are not 21. You're younger than my son, and he's only 18" she said.

"No no, you've got it wrong" I said. But then I noticed that Wasim was saying nothing, and his face had gone red. His mother had told us he was 21, but it seemed to have been another lie.

"So you're really only 17?" I said to him. I couldn't believe it.

My aunt laughed out loud. "Don't tell me you didn't know!" she said. I said nothing. She realised I was upset, so she changed the subject.

I sat there for a while thinking about what I had just found out. I didn't want them thinking how stupid or naive I was. Age may not matter if you are in love, but this hadn't been about love, it was about finding a decent, intelligent man who could be a good father for my daughter and a good husband for me.

I tried to behave as if I didn't really care what his age was, but it was killing me. When we got home Wasim went to the shops, and I took the opportunity to tell my parents what I had found out.

"So what's wrong with that, he is your husband now!" said my father. "But they lied about his age" I said. "He is only a child himself. How would he look after my daughter?"

My father stood up, red in the face. "What's wrong with you? I'm not going to hear this nonsense from you!" he shouted.

I knew that if I went on arguing with him things would get out of hand. But I told my mother about his affair. "These things happen" she said. She told me I was getting worried for no reason.

That night I slept with Henna while Wasim slept on another bed in the same room. In the middle of the night he woke me up. He seemed angry. "Who does your father think I am?" he said. I felt very scared and could feel my whole body shaking.

"What do you mean? What did he do?" I asked.

"I am not his servant or his gardener!" he shouted. "Who does he think he is, sending me to get cigarettes for him?"

The next morning he wouldn't talk to me, though he was being nice to my parents. I had got all my daughter's belongings with me and got ready to leave. My parents wanted her to stay with them, but I knew I couldn't have survived without her. She was my world, the only thing that was mine and the only person who loved me for who I was.

On the way home I kept thinking about what Wasim had said to me in the night. I couldn't understand why he wasn't talking to me. Was it because I had slept with Henna and not him? Or that I had found out his real age? Or was it just what he said, that my father had sent him to the shops? My father treated him as one of his own sons and it was no big deal if he asked him to go to the shops for him.

One day I walked in to find Wasim going through my purse. When I asked him what he was doing he said he was looking for a pen, but he had my money in his hand. There was a bundle of 25,000 rupees in there, worth about £250, given to me by my mother.

He realised I had seen him. "I was counting your money," he said. He threw the bag on the bed and grabbed me by the neck. "I'm your husband and I have a right to know!"

Things got worse. Sometimes he would slap me in anger. After a while I discovered that he was even hurting Henna when I wasn't there. I would find her crying because he had pinched her or grabbed her. He didn't want her there, of course. He wanted me to himself.

One day when I was cooking, my scarf caught fire. I rushed outside and tried to tear it off. I managed it, but the strange thing was that my husband saw the whole thing from his chair in the garden and didn't move an inch to help me.

I didn't know what to do. I knew I wasn't going to get any support from my family or my parents and I was too weak to do anything by myself. My husband's family were nice to me, but the truth was that they had used me to get a better life for their son, an immature young man whose anger they could not control.

I threw myself into housework and started to look after the home for the family. It kept me busy, and I earned praise from my in-laws. My sister-in-law found her clothes all ironed and hanging out ready for her. We became good friends, but when it came to my husband and me of course they all supported him. They shouted at him sometimes, but they could not make him change his behaviour. I decided to let Henna stay with my parents while we were in Pakistan, because they loved her and I knew that she was safe with them.

My mother-in-law was so insensitive. In front of friends she would say, "We kept the good one and got rid of the shit one!"

CHAPTER 4

The next year I returned to England, and stayed with my parents. I kept telling my mother what my husband was like and what he had done, but all she could say was "What would people say? They will blame you. You will ruin your daughter's future if you try to get out of your second marriage." She may have been right.

I never said anything to my father. I was just happy that he was talking to me nicely now and I didn't want to get him angry again.

Wasim insisted that I phone him regularly and would keep me on the phone a long time. If I ever missed calling him he would get angry and tell me what he would do to me.

At night I would lie awake crying with worry, wondering what would happen to me and my daughter.

When he went for his interview for a visa I hoped so much that somehow he wouldn't get one and Henna and I would be safe from him in England. But a few days later the phone rang, and my father shouted to me in excitement. "Shahnaz!" shouted my father. "Great news, he got his visa!"

My parents really thought I would be excited at the news. They had no idea. They did not understand, or want to.

One of my friends asked me why I didn't just run away. But I couldn't do that. My father would have hunted me down and killed me. And I would never do that to them - they were my parents who had respect in the community.

I was told that when Wasim arrived we would be moving in

with my older brother-in-law, who was married to my aunt. They gave me a nice room. My aunt and I were childhood friends, but I was very disappointed that she had not told me the truth about my husband.

For his arrival I wore a new brown dress, which I had made myself. My aunt had taught me to sew.

When we met Wasim at the airport he looked very smart and handsome in a new three-piece suit. He looked pleased to see me and shook my hand and asked how I was. I didn't feel scared, not yet anyway.

When we got home visitors started to come one by one, in the way of Asian families. They backbite all the time about each other, but when they get together it's as if they would die for each other. My aunt and I made tea all evening for the succession of guests. My parents came along with my daughter, and my husband was nice to her and kissed and cuddled her and gave her some gifts.

That day my daughter wanted to go with my younger brother, as he had promised her a doll. I didn't mind, as I wanted to see how my husband was going to be with me. That night he was fine. We talked for a while and then fell asleep. But in the morning he started to ignore me again.

My aunt promised to talk to him. She knew his past. In fact she probably knew things about him I didn't know.

I started to do the vacuuming as she went to talk to him. As I switched it off I heard him say "I'm with her all night, what else does she want?" He knew I was listening – I was right there in front of him. I wanted to slap his face, but of course I didn't dare.

That night he did to me what he wanted, without asking me or talking to me, then he just fell asleep. I felt like a used doll, or worse, a whore.

The next morning I decided to sit down and talk to him and ask him what I had done wrong to be treated like this. But he was one step ahead of me. He got ready to leave with my aunt instead. I went back to the cleaning.

In the evening I put Henna to bed and waited for Wasim to come up. When I said we needed to talk, he made an excuse about having to brush his teeth and then disappeared downstairs. In the end I went down and told him I was waiting, but still he wouldn't come up and talk to me.

At last he came into the bedroom and asked me what I wanted.

"I just wanted to know what I had done wrong for you to not talk to me."

"I just don't feel like talking to you."

"I don't understand. You're the one who has been treating me badly. You have been hitting me and treating me badly and now you're not talking to me."

He went wild. He pushed me off the bed and started to kick me in the ribs. I begged him to leave me alone, but he carried on kicking me and swearing at me and my family. My daughter woke up and started to cry.

"Shut your mouth and go sleep," he shouted at her.

Then God gave me some strength. I got up and shouted out

"Don't you dare shout at her." I hugged her and told her it was OK.

My aunt came in and dragged him out of the room. She asked if I was OK. I just kept crying. She hugged me and cried with me, but what could she do?

That night Wasim slept in the other room. The next morning he said he was sorry. He had just lost control. I said nothing. I just stayed quiet.

Life was becoming very difficult for my little daughter. She became very upset whenever I left my parents' house to go home, even though it was only a few minutes' drive away. I would call her as soon as I got home, but she would scream and cry "Mummy!" I would put the phone down and cry in the bathroom for hours without anyone knowing. For years her screams stayed in my head. What had I or my daughter done to be going through all this, I thought?

There was another reason I didn't bring my daughter into this house. Every time she came, my brother-in-law would take his son into his room and keep him there until Henna had gone. Why would he do that? What harm could a four-year-old girl have done to him? I started to hate these people, but I had no choice but stay with them.

I would clean the house and look after their children – I didn't mind doing that, because I loved them as if they were my own. I remember once the little girl asked for some cereal and I gave her some, just as I would for my own little Henna. Such a little thing, but it made me start crying and I wept until I had no more tears left.

One sunny day we all went to my parents' house for Eid, a time when all Muslims celebrate. My husband didn't want to come. He joined us in the end, but started telling me I had to be back that evening, although I had wanted to stay over.

For once I left Henna happily playing as she had her cousins with her to distract her.

When I got home I went up to bed and found Wasim appeared to be asleep, but I soon realised he was only pretending. He asked me to switch the light on, so I got up, switched it on and got back into bed. A few minutes later he asked me to switch it off again. I did so.

"Why did you turn the light off?" he asked.

"You told me to."

"No I didn't."

"But you did!"

"Get up and switch it on!" he said. I got up again and switched it back on, but by now I knew he was playing some sort of game with me.

Then he asked me to massage his back by standing on it. I was very tired, but of course I agreed. You can't say no to your husband.

As I stood on his back he wriggled.

"Stay still, I'm going to fall," I said. But he started to wiggle again and I nearly fell on to the floor.

Then he said he wanted to talk to me, so I sat up.

"Do you know, my life is like a game of cards?" he said. What was he talking about?

"I can take you in the dark and put a rope around your neck

35

and finish you without anyone knowing" he said. "I have the rope. I took it from your father's cellar."

I knew he was telling the truth - my father did have a thick red rope in the cellar. I started to pray in my heart "Oh God please help, help me get though this!" I could feel the tears coming, tears of fear.

Then he asked me: "So tell me, how was the first night with your first husband?"

"Why are you asking such things?" I said.

"Look in the mirror" he said. "You think you are pretty? Well, to me you're a donkey's ass." I thought, I never said I was pretty, why is he saying all this? I didn't understand what I could have done to this man to make him behave like this towards me.

"How long did you stay with your first husband?"

I was shaking badly now. "Nearly two years."

"So how long are you planning to stay with me?"

He pulled my hair and told me I must tell him I would stay with him forever. I was too scared to say anything else.

"Forever" I said.

"Oh no you're not. I'm divorcing you."

He kept swearing at me and telling me he would kill me. I started to lose it. I got so out of control that I started banging a mug on my head. (I wish now I had banged it on his head instead). Then I banged my head on the wall. I was screaming and crying. Then he started trying to calm me down, saying he was joking.

By now his brother and my aunt had walked into the room, but it was Wasim who tried to call an ambulance. I heard my brother-in-law shouting at him. Are you mad?" he was saying. "Send her to hospital in this state and you will be trouble."

I can't remember much else about that night. I do remember waking up and feeling lost. I was at my grandmother's house, my aunt's mother. My mother called to tell me that she was going to send my brother to pick me up.

It seems my aunt and sister-in-law had realised something was wrong with me the next day, because I was saying things that didn't make sense and couldn't manage even the simplest tasks. They said my brother-in-law had sent Wasim to his sister's house.

My family looked after me. Wasim's brother got very upset and begged me to forgive him. "We treated you badly," he said. "We wanted to give you happiness, but we were in the wrong."

Finally I went back home. When my husband appeared, my brother-in-law shouted at him in front of me, telling him not to bother me if I didn't want to talk to him.

I stayed in my room that day away from him, but at night he forced himself upon me and I could not stop him. The next morning I told my aunt, and after that I heard slaps and swearing going on in the living room.

Then I was told to go back to my parents' house and get some documents I had left there - they needed his National Insurance number. I went with my husband to the appointment at the Job Centre and got his NI number sorted.

My aunt helped him to find a job in a bakery and he started leaving early each morning to work there. This gave me a chance to go to my parents' house and spend time with my daughter each day.

One day there came a phone call from the bakers to say there had been an accident. My husband had cut off part of his finger and had been rushed off in an ambulance. My brother-in-law drove us to the hospital.

He had to wait two days for an operation. He would scream with pain and shout at me and squeeze my hand violently, and I would share his pain as my rings pressed into my fingers. He kept sending me off to ask why they weren't operating on him yet, and each time they told me children were the first priority. Then he would shout at me that I wasn't trying hard enough. I thought, he is a child too, the youngest child in the ward.

When it was time to leave hospital they showed me how to replace his bandage. I changed it every four hours. For three months he would make me do everything for him, even give him a bath and take his socks off. My aunt told him he was being childish. It was only a finger, after all. Eventually it healed and he found a new job working in a store.

My aunt was leaving the country with her children so that their grandparents could see them. One day some visitors came to see her. One of them saw Henna and asked who she was. I was just about to say she was my daughter when Wasim made a sign to me not to say anything. But I was not going to deny that she was my daughter just because someone didn't like it.

"She's mine," I said.

"But you have only been married two years" said the lady. I realised that they did not know that Wasim was the second asshole I had been married to.

"She was married before, poor girl," said my aunt. There was an awkward silence. Wasim looked very annoyed. I took Henna by the hand and led her into the kitchen. He followed me there.

"Why the hell did you have to say that, you bitch?" he hissed in my ear.

"She is my daughter! How can I deny it?" I replied. He swore at me and walked away.

CHAPTER 5

One day I found out I was pregnant. Of course, it wasn't planned. When I was seven months gone I had to be rushed into hospital with abnormal pains. The doctors did some scans and it was soon obvious that something was badly wrong. They sent me to a hospital in London, where they discovered that my baby's brain had stopped growing.

The baby died in the womb four days later. Giving birth to it was very painful. My older sisters and the other ladies of the family were with me, and the hospital gave me a special room.

The day I was to leave the hospital I called my mother and asked her to send my brother Zaid to pick me up. But then my husband and brother-in-law turned up to collect me. I told them I was going with Zaid. They were annoyed, but I didn't really care what they thought. I stayed and waited for my brother.

At home my mother had prepared a bed for me downstairs so that I could be with everyone. My daughter was very happy to see me.

Then the phone rang. It was my brother-in-law, asking why I was not at their house. "What's wrong with you?" said my mother. "She is in no state to be left alone! Don't you understand what has happened to her?"

I told my mother that whatever happened, I was not going back. My father agreed that I needed the rest, and said that my husband could come to our house if he wanted.

Wasim stayed with us for a while, but he was constantly jealous of me and Henna. If I was doing something with her he would call me to do a job for him. He would insist I do some job when I was in the middle of reading her a bedtime story, and then when I went back to her she would have gone to sleep on her own, waiting for me.

I was still very scared of him. If he called me on my mobile for something and I was out shopping he would go mad and demand that I should come straight back home. Sometimes I just had to leave my shopping in the trolley and leave. When I got home I would often find he was waiting in the cellar to see if I was up to anything. We would argue about this and he would beat me up for no reason, even in front of my daughter.

Wasim would say that I was like a shoe, because my place was under his feet. He kept saying that women were there to be used and abused by men. Next time, he said, he was going to get married to a virgin.

One day when my daughter had gone to stay overnight with my parents, he put a chair in the middle of the room and told me to sit on it. I got frightened, but he just laughed. He said he wanted to talk to me.

As soon as I sat on the chair, he tied me up. I tried to get away but couldn't. Then he went to the kitchen. When he came back he was holding a knife.

He put the knife on the table and asked who I had been phoning. I didn't understand what he was saying. "Nobody!" I said. He repeated a few phone numbers and asked me who they belonged to. I told him – they were all just friends or family. He called the numbers, just to make sure. Once he was satisfied he untied me and laughed.

"I was only joking with you," he said. He put the knife back in the kitchen. After that he started to be nicer to me, but every time he touched me I wanted to get that knife and stick it in his ass.

My mother still didn't understand what was going on or what I was going through. She didn't want to understand. I told her everything that had happened, but she did nothing. She just kept saying that maybe I was in the wrong, perhaps I was doing things that were making him suspicious.

During one argument Wasim threw a glass on the floor and smashed it. Then he hit me and threw me across the room. I cut my hand badly and blood kept gushing out. My daughter was crying. I tried to run for the phone, but he stopped me.

Henna ran into the garden. I ran after her and tried to comfort her, and just then the phone rang. It was my father. I heard Wasim telling him I was out.

I knew I had to get away from this man soon, before it was too late.

One morning he said something about his brother that provoked me - I can't remember what it was. I said, "I don't give a damn about your brother. Who does he think he is?" That was the first time I ever really dared to shout at him. He started to kick me and threw a shoe at me. I kept saying I was sorry and begging him to stop but then he slapped me so hard that I saw stars. Then he took off his belt and hit me with it several times. I sat on the floor and sobbed until I could cry no more.

The next day a friend of mine came round and saw the bruises from the belt. She told my sister, who took me home to my parents. My mother saw the bruises, but still she didn't really take any notice. When Wasim came to take me home he promised her he wouldn't touch me again. My mother took him at his word and told me I should go with him.

That was when I decided to leave.

I called a women's refuge. The lady there answered my call in a soothing voice. She didn't seem to mind that I could hardly get my words out. I started to tell her what had happened. She told me to come to the refuge as soon as I could. My husband was at work, so I was able to pack my things and leave. I had my mobile ready to dial 999, just in case he turned up.

The refuge was in a hidden location and no-one had access to the building. The other women were nice to me and I was nice to them. We had all been through the same thing. I stayed there for several months.

While I was at the refuge I got friendly with a man I knew called Azam who ran a family shop we used. He had noticed my bruises. He had seen me carrying heavy bottles of water to put in our car radiator because my husband would not carry them. He had also seen him shouting at me in the middle of the road, and worse, he had seen him shout at Henna when she asked for some of his chocolate. Wasim had told her to shut her mouth or he would knock her into the road. When I think of that day I feel like killing him, even now.

I started to go to see Azam and we became friends. He gave me his number and told me that if I ever needed help I should call him straight away. He felt sorry for me, and his kindness made me feel very close to him. I had never had that from any man before. Azam was the only one who would listen, the only one who could see what I was going through. But he said I would have to deal with my situation myself, because no-one else could do it.

Eventually someone saw me and my family and worked out where I was living. One day my brother Bilal called me. I didn't usually answer the phone, but I didn't mind speaking to him. He told me my father understood what I had gone through and was willing to take me back home. They didn't think it was right for me to be living in a refuge.

I didn't want to leave the safety of the refuge, but they started to put pressure on me. Sheana had to have an operation, and my mother phoned and said, what kind of sister was I not to go and see her? Wasim would call and leave horrible messages for me.

I went to see Sheana and took her some flowers. Then I plucked up the courage to visit my parents' house. I got a warm welcome from my family. But when I stood up to go back to the refuge my father wouldn't have it. He wanted me to stay there. In the end they persuaded me to come back and live with them. They made me feel it would be wrong not to let my daughter live a good life in a proper house with them.

So the following day I collected my stuff from the refuge and moved in with my family. I went back to cleaning and cooking, with my sister-in-law helping. That was all I did. I was not allowed to go out alone except to take my daughter to school. It was just like the old days, before I was married.

My father couldn't forget that I had run away from my husband. To him it was a crime. He would shout at me. My parents refused to understand why I had had no choice but to run away.

By now my big brother Shan was married and had moved out of the family home. Zaid was also married and was still living with my parents. Zaid would not take any disrespect for his family in front of his wife, so he did not support me either.

I started to call my friend Azam more often, as he seemed to be the only one who could help me to get through this, the only one who was listening to me without judging me. He was a goods friend.

One day when I went to collect Henna from school I saw Wasim. He came up to talk to me. Henna got frightened. We started to walk fast to get away from him. I told him I didn't want to talk to him, but he followed us all the way home. He only gave up when we got to the house.

My parents were concerned, as they could see how scared Henna was. She was panting with fear. Then my father started shouting at me. Why had I gone to collect her from school in the first place? "I'm her mother, who else will?" I said.

"You're not going any more, not even to drop her off!" he shouted.

"I'm not stopping because of him!" I said. I went into my room with Henna.

My father ran upstairs and charged into my room. His eyes were red and blazing. He was about to grab me and slap me when my mother came in between us. "Look who's in the room!" she said. Henna started to cry and soon we were both crying. I had never seen my father as angry as this.

Then my mother started to shout at me. Why did I want to go out when my father had said I was not allowed out any more? It was the old story – my father's word was law, whatever he said, however unfair it was.

"She's my daughter! She needs me!" I said. My father heard and came back into the room. He started shouting again. My mother tried to push him away, but he went on shouting and screaming at me. I just sat there on the bed, but now I wasn't crying – I must have been in shock. I wasn't going to be allowed out and I wasn't even going to be allowed to use the phone. They were making me a prisoner.

One day Wasim phoned. He wanted to talk to me, but I said I wasn't ready. He got angry and started to swear and call me a whore and a bitch. He swore at me, my daughter, even my mother and father.

Then he stopped, and it was my turn. I swore right back. I said I had had enough of him and everyone in his household. I even called his mother a bitch. I don't know what came over me. I had never in my life sworn like that before. Until then, all I had ever seemed to say to those around me was "sorry".

I put the phone down and sat on the sofa in the living room to calm down. My mother came down to ask what had happened as she had heard me shouting. Nothing, I said.

Then my father walked in. He was carrying a broom from the kitchen and looked as if he was going to hit me with it. I was terrified. My whole body started shaking. He grabbed me by the arm and threw me on the floor. My mother and brother tried to stop him.

"She's a bitch!" he said. He had heard the phone call. He had heard me swearing about my husband and all his family. Wasim must have told my father to listen in to the phone call, but only after he had finished swearing about them himself.

My father didn't hit me with the broomstick. He just told me to get out of his sight. I got up and walked slowly past them and up the stairs, the same familiar stairs I knew so well, to the top floor. Same old house, same old floors and same old me, but so much had happened since I used to sit on the floor outside my sisters' room and wish I was allowed inside.

After that I was told I would not be allowed out of my room. What a way to treat a grown woman, a mother, who had been through so much because of what other people had done. My life was not making any kind of sense. I thought, I have been through all that, and my father thinks I am dirt.

One day my mother came into my room to talk to me. I hated her at that time as she was knew that it was wrong for me to be treated that way, but she let it happen. She told me how wicked I was to speak my mind and not to listen to my father.

"I'm not a little girl any more," I said. "I want to live my own life."

Then Zaid came rushing in. He had been listening.

"Why are you arguing with your mother?" he shouted.

"I'm just talking to her" I said.

"You're not just talking, I can hear you!" he said. And he slapped me across my face, three times. This was my brother, the brother I loved to bits, the one who knew what I had gone through. He had witnessed my dreadful life, and now he was hitting me. He was showing his wife what a man he was to hit his older sister.

I just sat there and took the blows. I suppose he had the right to show off in front of his wife.

Then my father walked in. There was silence.

"What the hell is she saying now?" he said.

Oh God, I prayed, please not today, I can't bear it any more. I felt like jumping out of the window, but I always thought of my daughter. Thank God she was at school.

"Listen to me, girl! You pack your bags and get out of here! We are sick of you!"

"I must get downstairs, now" I thought. I got up and went to pick up my scarf, as I never walked around the house without it, but I think father thought I was starting to pack my stuff.

He hit me on the face, three times.

"I'm only picking up my scarf!" I cried out. How strange to think that I still had so much respect for my father that I didn't want to be in his presence without a scarf on.

He didn't say anything. He just left the room.

I had had two mobile phones, one of them given to me by Azam. I had hidden them in case I needed them, but my mother had found them both and smashed them, so I couldn't communicate with anyone.

I can't remember much about the time after that. My nights

and days all seemed to run together. Somehow I knew I had to get out, but it was impossible. Everyone was watching me.

Then I had an idea. For once, I used my brain. I wrote a letter to my daughter's teacher. I couldn't write very well because I was shaking with fear in case anyone found out. I made a lot of mistakes, because of course I had had to stop going to school when I was 12 and my spelling was very bad.

I put the letter in Henna's bag without my family knowing, and whispered to her to give it to her teacher. I begged her not to show it to anyone else.

A few days later, I heard a noise outside – the sound of police walkie-talkies. Then there was a knock on the door of my room, and in came three police officers.

The officers looked shocked at the state I was in. I had a bruise on my face near my eyes and I was very pale and weak.

They wanted to speak to me in private, but I was shaking so much that I couldn't talk. They kept telling me everything would be fine. One of the officers went and spoke to my father. He didn't try to stop them taking me. "If that's what she wants, fine," he said. I knew my father wasn't going to start any trouble with the police, as to him respect was everything.

I piled all my stuff into some black plastic bags and walked downstairs. My family were all there watching. I didn't look at them. I asked the woman police officer to stand right next to me so I didn't have to face any of them.

As I was about to walk out, a bag of clothes fell from my hands. "Leave it, I don't need these clothes," I told her. I did need them, of course. She knew I was too scared – I just wanted to get out.

She helped me to put the clothes back into the bag. I looked into the kitchen and saw my father standing there. I had loved and cared for this man all my life, but I could not live with his rules and regulations. He was refusing to understand what I had gone through because of them. I had never wanted this to happen, never wanted to challenge my father's respect, but I had no choice. He just stood there, one hand on the kitchen worktop. I could see he was in despair. I hated having to do this to my family, but they had put us all in this position.

CHAPTER 6

I picked my daughter up from school and was taken to another women's refuge. It was a long drive. The officers were very nice and helpful. They took a statement and asked me to make a complaint about the people who had caused grief to me, but I could not, because they were my family and I still loved them despite everything.

I stayed in the refuge for several months. I had no contact with any of my family. My daughter had changed schools, and she started to miss them. She kept crying and asking me to call them, and in the end I agreed.

My younger brother Bilal answered the phone. He was amazed to hear my voice. "Oh my god, how are you?" he said. He sounded very emotional. I was in tears too.

We talked for a while, but he didn't ask me where I was. Then my daughter spoke to him, and she burst into tears and told him she was missing everyone. My brother told me that everyone was missing me and my father didn't want anyone to look for me. He understood that I didn't want to see them. After that I started to call my brother quite often and let my daughter speak to him. I spoke to my brother Qasim as well.

I then left the refuge and moved into a flat. I spent what money I had doing it up. I met up with Bilal a couple of times outside the area. He would mostly come with his friend, who was like another brother to me.

The first time we saw him Henna was overjoyed with happiness. She wouldn't stop talking to him. He would get her loads of stuff and gifts for me and we would have meals together. He would tell me that our father was hating himself for treating me badly. I found it hard to believe that, but it was true that father had not searched for me, even though they knew my brother was coming to see me now and then.

When I was sure it was safe I let Bilal into the house. It wasn't fair on my daughter to stop her seeing him, as she was very close to him. Soon he started to stay overnight.

One day when I knew my father was not home, I went to visit my mother. My other two brothers didn't want to know me, as they said I had disgraced the family by running away.

One day I walked into my daughter's room to find her sitting on the prayer mat the way my mother did. She had her hands up in the air and was crying. I realised she was praying to God. I felt very disturbed, because to see a young girl crying to God was unusual. I did not interrupt her, but once she was done I called her to me. She didn't want to come to me, so I went close to her and asked her what she was asking for.

"I was praying to God because I want to be with my family," she said. "I have nobody here. My friends get to see their families, but I don't."

"Have you forgotten what our family did to me?" I said. "They would kill me now if I went back."

"But they are our family! We can't live without them!" she cried. God help me, I thought, what should I do now?

She started to make a scene and cry for my parents, so in the end I asked my brother to take her there. After that she started to miss school and stay with them.

I was completely stuck. Henna was everything I had.

I then asked Bilal to ask my father to get me a divorce, as I didn't want anything more to do with Wasim. He agreed and my divorce came through a few months later. My younger brothers started to take me back home more often, and sometimes I would stay overnight. My father was fine with me and seemed to have accepted that I had my own life to live.

Then my mother asked me to go with her to Pakistan, but I refused. She said people were talking and the respect they had built up was going down the drain. All she wanted was for me to go with her for a month. She just wanted to show people I was still around and had not run away with anyone.

I kept saying no, and she kept begging and crying – it was emotional blackmail. Bilal said he would come with me and bring me back. I trusted my brother to do as he said as he had kept his word up till now, so finally I agreed. My parents were delighted.

At the airport in Pakistan a driver came to pick us up. It was early and people were busy going off to work. I could hear the birds singing. It was a beautiful morning.

In Pakistan the days went past pleasantly and peacefully. My brother and I would go out every day and spent money like water - father had given mother a lot of money for us. We would drive up into the mountains and go to a restaurant high up which had beautiful views. We would leave tips of 300 or 500 rupees, which was a lot of money – no wonder they liked serving us! Sometimes we took with us two sisters who lived next door, Robi and Banu.

When we had eaten we would go to the shopping mall under the restaurant, where they had everything you can get in the malls in London.

Sometimes we would ask the driver to drive around so we could do some sightseeing - we were only there for a month, so we wanted to make the most of it. My daughter asked a million questions about the country.

One day I woke up to find my brother in my room. He was taking his passport from the drawer where all the passports were locked. When I asked him what he was doing with it he said he was taking it to sort the seats out for the return flight.

"What about mine?" I asked him.

"You can sort it out later, I need to go, I have to go to college" he said.

I got out of bed and tried to follow him, but he left in a hurry. I quickly went to wash myself. While I was in the bath I began to feel something was very wrong. Why were they taking their passports and not mine? I felt scared and lost. I didn't know what to do. "Please God, don't let it be what I think," I thought. Surely they would not play more games with me?

My daughter was still fast asleep in her bed, still in her angel world. Outside my mother was sitting in the sun preparing vegetables. I was very scared, but I had to ask her the question that was on my mind. I dreaded what the reply would be.

"When are we going back?" I asked her.

"Why?" said my mother. Then she looked at me in a strange way. "You're not going anywhere."

It was just what I had dreaded. They would not let me go back to England because I had ignored my father's wishes and dragged down the family name. Then she started lecturing me again about my behaviour.

I can still remember those words and the look my mother gave me. I hated her so much. "You wicked, evil woman!" I thought. I wanted to scream, but all I could do was cry.

"What about my daughter and her education?" I asked her.

"She can go to school here," she said, and she got up and walked away.

I sat there on the grass. I was shocked at what they were capable of doing to their daughter just because she had tried to make one or two choices of her own.

I looked up at the sky. "Are you really up there, God?" I asked.

I waited for my brother to come back home - he had so many questions to answer. When he came back he didn't come to my room as he usually would. I called him and in he came. I asked him what was going on.

"You will be coming back, but I need to go first" he said. "I promise you they aren't going to leave you here. They will bring you back."

He looked confused himself and I knew he was lying. I begged him to take me with him, but he wouldn't say anything. Perhaps he thought I was better off here.

"England is my home, not Pakistan," I said. "My daughter needs to be there too. What have I done so wrong to be punished like this?" But he would not listen.

My mother was very religious. She would pray five times a day and bath five times day. She would always answer my questions by referring to God. I was praying myself, but I never understood the holy Qu'ran as it was in Arabic. Every day we read our prayers five times on the mat and every morning we read the Qu'ran.

My mother would always say that the women were lower than the men and we should obey everything the men said. So wrong! Later on I studied what the Qu'ran really says, and learned that in fact Islam does not differentiate women so much from men. Women have as much right as men to fight for their rights, as long as they do not commit a sin. Women have every right to decide who they want to marry. We were told we have to cover ourselves in front of our fathers, brothers and uncles all the time – wrong again! The Qu'ran does not say that – it is the men who have made these rules.

The Qu'ran does say that you should not force a divorcee to marry against her wishes. It also says that you should not marry your daughters to men who do not follow God, or force a divorcee to marry against her wishes. Here are a couple of passages from the Qu'ran to show what it really says:

"I shall not lose sight of the labour of any of you who labours in My way, be it man or woman; each of you is equal to the other." (Chapter 3:195).

"It is not lawful for you that you should take women as heritage against (their) will, and do not straiten them in order that you may take part of what you have given them, unless they are guilty of manifest indecency, and treat them kindly; then if you hate them, it may be that you dislike a thing while Allah has placed abundant good in it." (Chapter 4.19).

How these people had emotionally blackmailed me and dragged me into this hell! And all because they were obsessed with 'respect'. They had imprisoned me and lied to me. They did not care about their children, only their own stupid 'respect'. How could they do that to their own daughter!

Once my brother had left I had no-one to talk to. I wasn't even allowed out, as there was no-one to take me anymore.

Then my father came back. He walked in through the door and my daughter ran to him. I took a deep breath and walked towards him. I didn't know how he was going to behave, so I went up to him while the driver was standing beside him, because I knew he would not behave badly to me when other people were there. I said hello and hugged him, and he hugged me in return. That made me a little less afraid. He sat down, looking happy to see us. Once he had taken a shower and eaten, he talked normally to me and Henna.

But as the days went past my father became more distant. Mother and father would talk without involving me. I would try to join in the conversation, but they would take no notice, so I would just go to my room or wander round the garden.

At first I kept asking my mother when I would be going back, but she always got cross with me, so after a while I stopped asking. I did have a mobile phone, and I was able to call my friend Azam. Azam was very fond of me and he told me he had missed me. He also said he wanted to marry me. He said he would come to my parents and ask for my hand in marriage. But he was in no position to do such a thing - he was already married and had children!

He said he loved me too much to let me go. He wanted to give me a good life and show me what married life could be. He said he could not live with his wife and they had been having problems for a long time. He said she was treating him badly. He was going to leave her soon, and then he would come to ask for my hand. Perhaps it was all true, but even if it was, he still could not marry me.

And yet I so badly wanted someone who would love me and care for me, because so far all those who had claimed they loved me had betrayed me. I would think about Azam's wife and feel sorry for her, but I was thinking about myself too. When I called him he always seemed to be with his children and they sounded as if they were having a happy time. It made me think he would be a good father for my daughter, which was what I thought she really needed.

My father and mother still couldn't help showing their anger that I had left home twice. And now they started bringing people who wanted me to marry their sons! I knew that all these men wanted was the precious red passport. I would just leave the room and show them that I wasn't interested.

My mother would tell me I should get married again. She would tell me it was the only way to be happy, the only way to make my father happy. She would talk to me for hours and hours about it, and my answer would always be – no, I will not get married again. Then she would say, fine, then you will die here! She would walk away and refuse to talk to me for the rest of the day. I would be left all alone, because my daughter would sit with them, not knowing any better.

One evening my daughter and I were sitting around with some of my cousins, joking and bantering. I sent one of the workers to get samosas and drinks and we all ate the hot food together. Then after a while the cousins got ready to leave, and my daughter said she wanted to go with them. I said she could not, and my parents told her the same, but she wouldn't accept it. She started to cry and cling on to them. In the end they left without her, and she would not stop crying. I tried to calm her down, but she wouldn't listen.

Then my mother started to shout at me. She said I didn't know how to look after my daughter and she was as bad as her mother. I felt very angry. I grabbed Henna by the arm and took her from the room. I tried to shut the door behind me, but my father rushed up behind me and pushed me to the floor. He started to kick my stomach and slapped and punched me. I was screaming. The staff heard the noise and they all came running into the room and tried to pull him away, but my father just kept on hitting me. Henna was sobbing and telling him to stop, but no-one could stop father when he was angry.

"She needs to learn!" shouted my father. "She thinks she can do what she likes!" I just sat on the floor.

In the end everyone left the room, leaving me there alone on the floor. One of the female staff came in and sat next to me, crying with me and hugging me. Why couldn't my mother do that!

"I don't understand - why did he hit you?" she asked. "You weren't even doing anything wrong!"

I asked her to leave for a while, as I wanted to be alone. My daughter came in and sat next to me and said she was sorry, but of course it wasn't her fault. She said I had a bruise on my face.

Then I heard the doorbell. One of the staff came in to tell me that one of my uncles and two ladies had come - these were the people who had been asking for my hand for their son. They were very poor, as the boy's father had died.

I managed to get up and go to the mirror. There was a terrible bruise on my face and my eyes were red and swollen. I washed my face, but I couldn't wash the bruise away.

They started to call for me. I tried hiding the bruise with my hair and scarf, but try as I might I couldn't cover it up. I had to come out as I was, as I didn't want to annoy my father again. I didn't have the strength to get beaten like an animal any more.

I walked into the hallway where my mother was sitting with the women. My father was with the men in the other room, thank goodness. I didn't want to look at anyone because I knew I would burst out crying.

One of the ladies asked me what had happened to my face. My mother spoke before I could say anything. "Her father got angry with her because of her daughter" she said. The women did not understand. One of them said it was not nice to shout at a daughter, and especially one who was married with a child, but my mother just laughed it off.

I was afraid I was going to start crying again, so I got up to leave the room. One of the women had her daughter with her, so I asked the daughter to come to my room. We sat and chatted and I asked her what her brothers did for a living. She said two of them had hairdressing salons and the other two were carpenters.

My parents took me to their house a couple of times after that. They were nice people but very poor. The young man, Nazir, seemed very nice and straightforward. His mother was too embarrassed to take us to their house, but my mother insisted. She told her it didn't matter what sort of house you lived in as long as you were all happy with each other – I couldn't believe that, coming from my mother! She could be nice enough with other people.

When we went to their house they had four rooms and a nice kitchen, but she was too shy to show us the toilet. She said they were repairing it. Her husband had died and Nazir and his brother had been looking after the house since they were 10 and 12 years old. Then she started to cry. I felt very sorry for her. My mother comforted her.

My father really wanted me to get married to one of these boys and he kept trying to talk me into it. I would just laugh, but inside I was thinking that perhaps this was the only way I was going to get away from him.

I was still very scared, because my mother had told me father would kill me and anyone else who tried to get involved in my life. All I wanted was to get away from them. I had started to hate them so much I couldn't bear to be in the same room.

One day I called Azam on his mobile. He was out shopping with his wife. To my surprise he was angry that I had called, and started to shout at me. He told me I was causing problems for him. I didn't understand this, as he had said he was having nothing to do with his wife and was just living with her for the sake of his family. I said I was sorry, but he just said goodbye and hung up. After this I felt very confused. I had trusted him and thought he was my only hope.

I stopped calling Azam after that, but I still got calls from him. I didn't answer them, as I knew now it was wrong.

One day I went to my mother and told her I was ready to get married again. She was amazed, but very pleased. She ran to father to tell him. I really didn't know what I was doing. One of the boys started doing some work in our house - I don't know if this was planned or not, but he started to come around more often.

I thought I should ring Azam and tell him I was planning to get married and didn't want to spoil his life any further. Again he said he was too busy to talk, because he was taking his children home from school. He said he would call me later, and put the phone down on me again. It was obvious he only wanted to talk to me when he was on his own. His family life sounded happy enough to me. By now I felt sure I was doing the right thing in ending our friendship.

My mother was happy and excited and my father was over the moon too. They started talking to me nicely. Suddenly I was their favourite daughter.

The family came once again to ask for my hand and this time my father accepted. Nazir's uncle, who was my uncle too, was laughing with excitement. I was always happy to make others happy.

My father rang home to the UK to tell them. My brother Shan called back and said he wanted to talk to me. I could hear my mother saying, "No no, she's happy, it's what she wants". When I took the phone, Shan asked me if this was my own decision. I said it was, although really what I wanted most was just to go back to England. I didn't want to stay in Pakistan and could not go on living with my parents. This marriage was the only way out.

"Are you sure no-one forced you?" said Shan. "Quite sure" I said. I was so glad that someone really seemed to care about me. My younger brother Bilal was shocked too.

That evening I saw that I had missed a call from Azam. I called back and told him I wasn't coming back to him and wanted him to be happy with his wife. He started to swear and shout at me - "you bitch! You slut!" Why was he saying this to me when I had known that he was happy with his wife?

"Just forget me!" I said. "I don't want anything more to do with you." It was my turn to put the phone down. I had never seen this side of him. He had never loved me after all.

I didn't do much shopping for my third marriage. I wanted to keep it simple. After all, it was quite embarrassing to be getting married for the third time.

My in-laws asked me if I wanted anything, but I told them there was nothing I needed. The wedding outfit cost 1000 rupees, which was about £10 in England.

The night before my wedding I didn't sleep. I stayed up watching two lizards on the wall. They didn't move an inch the whole night, which seemed very strange. I didn't move much either, just waiting for the next day.

I wasn't excited at all, I didn't feel there was anything to look forward to. But my daughter was very excited. She was just happy that she was going to wear new clothes.

We had just a normal ceremony, no fuss. I kept Henna beside me the whole day. Nazir was nice to her. He kept cuddling her and talking to her, which made us both happy. Perhaps now things would be better.

CHAPTER 7

We lived in my aunt's house next door to ours, which was nice because she had a daughter who got on well with Henna. My husband was good to me, and kept asking if I needed anything. He treated me like a queen, which was a change from what I had been used to. His mother was nice too - she would ask if I needed anything. I would say I didn't but she would not take no for an answer and would give me food. My brothers sent me gifts from England. My sister Rehanna had come out to Pakistan as she had family there and it was her brother-in-law who had arranged the match with my new husband.

But it wasn't long before there were storm clouds. Nazir's sister told me that he had been about to get married to a girl who lived two doors away and everything had been prepared for the wedding. He had known her for years and was so much in love with her that when his mother refused to let him marry her, he had pointed a gun at his head.

I didn't feel as much in shock as I might have done because of all that had happened to me, but it soon started to get to me as everywhere I went I kept hearing how much Nazir and this girl had loved each other. People would call him a Romeo. I would see her walking around on her roof and he would be watching her. I started getting jealous.

One day we went out on his motorbike. I wanted to go to a

park so I could talk to him properly. He never talked much if we went out - he would just sit there quietly and when I asked him questions he would just give one-word answers.

We sat on the grass and I told him what I had been hearing about him and the girl. At last he told me that yes, he had loved her. He got a little carried away and told me things I didn't really want to know. Then I saw tears in his eyes. I burst out crying myself. I couldn't tell him I had been involved with someone too and had had to give him up for the sake of my parents.

I kept asking him why he had never got married to the other girl, but he kept changing the subject. "Don't worry about it," he said.

But I needed to know. That night I asked him again why he hadn't married her. He smiled. "With her, my family don't have a very bright future" he said. "With you it will be much better."

Well, I had a straight answer. He had wanted to marry me for my family's money. I tried to go to sleep, but his words kept going around in my head.

After that we started to drift away from each other. How could he have said that to my face, even if it was true? Why couldn't I live with someone who really loved me for who I was and wouldn't just use me?

When I awoke the next day Nazir had gone. I got up and looked for him, and in the end I found him up on the roof. He was standing looking at the girl's balcony as usual, trying to see her. When he saw me he quickly turned the other way. I went straight to my room and sat on the sofa and he came and sat next to me giggling.

"I looked at her and she looked away," he said.

"I don't understand why you had go up there so early" I said. But I had got the picture. He had been ready to marry her, until I had come along. Then he had agreed to marry me instead, for my wonderful red British passport. He would be able to give his family a better life because no-one else in the family had lived away from Pakistan and they were living a very humble life. I felt deeply hurt, as I had done so much for him and had been through so much before. I wasn't sure I could take much more.

One evening when we were having dinner, my daughter as a joke kicked him softly. Nazir didn't say anything, and I was pleased with him because I thought he understood that she was only playing. Then a little later on Henna ran in to me crying and saying she wanted to go to my parents' house. I realised that Nazir had followed her out. I asked her what was wrong.

"Nazir told me that if I ever kicked him again he would throw you and me out of the house" she said.

Everyone went quiet. I sat there holding her in my arms. Then I burst into tears. My mother-in-law started to cuddle me and say Nazir was just being silly, I couldn't say anything.

Nazir came back into the room, looking like a different person. He ignored what everyone was saying to him and just went to bed. I calmed Henna down and took her back home to his aunt's house.

Neither of us spoke much the next day. I wanted to move back into my parents' house as my daughter was much happier there. I got my stuff ready and left and Nazir came to drop my stuff off.

A few days later we were all sitting together when one of my father's staff came to tell him someone had come to talk to him. My father went off to see who it was, looking a little worried. I went upstairs to see who had come and could see a white car outside and my father standing talking to someone.

After a while he came back in, looking upset and angry. He called my mother to the other room and they both talked in private for a while. Then they came out and told me to sit in front of them. My father was taking deep breaths and was looking very upset.

"He his here" said my father.

"Who is here?"

"Azam."

Azam was looking for me! They told me he had brought a gift for me, but they had refused to accept it. I felt completely lost. My mother told me that he had turned up the day I was getting married, knocking on doors and asking for me, but no-one had told him anything.

My head was spinning. I couldn't believe this. Why had Azam come all the way here for me? I was very frightened and didn't know what to do, what would happen next. What would happen to me? What would they do to Azam?

My father looked confused. He stared at the floor with his head in his hands. My mother sat quietly. Their calmness was more frightening than the shouting. At least with the shouting you knew where you were.

My father went up into his room and talked again in private

to my mother. They sent for one of the servants. After a while the servant came out and hurried past me without speaking.

Then my father left the house with the servant, who started to dig in the garden. I asked my mother what was going on. She told me my father wanted some work done in the garden. That seemed very strange. Why would father suddenly decide to have gardening work done, now?

My mother told me Azam was digging his grave by coming here like this. I was married and he was shaming the family. Were they digging his grave in the garden? I didn't know what to think.

When I went into the kitchen the chefs told me my father had ordered the work to be done so that the workers could watch out for anyone who tried to come into the house. He said they were carrying guns. That really freaked me out. My father had always hated weapons, I thought. Had I really pushed him that far?

The next day I spoke to my mother and suggested that I should call Azam's mother and tell him I was married and did not want anything more to do with him. Perhaps she would stop him trying to approach me. My mother was a little scared, but she agreed, and I made the call. At first Azam's mother swore at me, but then I started to cry and told her I had had enough. She said Azam had been very happy until I had come on the scene. She said he still loved his wife and was not going to let her go.

Eventually she gave me Azam's uncle's number and suggested I should call him. When I called him and explained it all, he said everything would be fine and that he would talk to him. But when I called him back to see what had happened, he said Azam had refused to listen. He said he loved me and had been crying his eyes out over me. He was refusing to give up hope of getting me back. When I heard that my heart skipped a beat.

He gave me a new number for Azam, which I hid from everyone. I decided to call him and tell him I had moved on and wanted nothing more to do with him.

When I called him, he cried and said that he loved me and would not let me go. I tried telling him that I was married and he was putting his life at risk, but he wouldn't listen. He kept saying he would do anything to get me back.

I told him not to come to the house and he made me promise I would call again.

What was I to do? I couldn't help thinking that Azam was the only person who could get me out of the country, who might be able to make me a free woman again. I called him again, and he said he was willing to take me away, out of the house.

That was when I started planning my escape. I was going to use Azam the way he and so many other men had used me. First I arranged for my daughter to fly back to England with a relative - I said to my father that she shouldn't be hanging around wasting time in Pakistan when she could be at school, and he had agreed. Then I called Azam and told him I was ready to leave with him.

My father never imagined I would try to run away to join Azam. He only thought that Azam would try to come to the house again for me. I started to stay away from Nazir, saying I wanted nothing to do with him as he had lied to me and used me.

I started to take my stuff round to my father's house. I left half my wedding money for my husband and his mother, as I knew they needed it more than I did. I also left some gold for my husband underneath his bed.

Friday was a special prayer day. The men were going to the mosque and the women would stay at home all day. The workers were going home to pray in their own mosques. Nazir was going as well. Before he went I sat next to him on the lawn, because I wanted to talk to him and in a way to say sorry to him. I kept saying I was sorry if I had said anything wrong to him, and that he should get married to the girl he loved, but he just giggled.

Once everyone had left I went to my room and stuffed all my things into three bags. Then I waited for Azam to ring me. My mother was praying in a room next to the door, so I had to jump from the wall into the house next door and then walk out through their gates. Our gates had big locks and it was impossible to leave that way without making any noise.

When the phone vibrated my heart started to race. I was feeling faint with fear. Pakistan must be the worst country in the world for a woman to try to run away, as everyone knows you and the news spreads like gas from a leaking pipe.

Azam said he was outside waiting. This was my only chance. If I didn't take it I knew things could only get worse for me. I would end up rotting away here in Pakistan.

I picked up my bags and slowly went out through the bathroom door. I could see my mother on the prayer mat. I took a deep breath and threw my bags over the wall. Then I climbed over after them.

Then I saw two friends of mine, two sisters, in the street. They had seen me. They ran towards me and asked what I was doing.

"I'm going back to London," I said. One of them got frightened and started to grab me. "Don't do it!" she begged. But no-one could stop me now. I told them to get off me and ran towards the gates. They stood there watching. One of them sat on the floor, shaking. She couldn't believe I was capable of doing this.

Azam was waiting there in a big white car with the engine running. I threw my bags in and he accelerated away. I looked back at my parents' mansion. Somehow it looked to me now as if it was going to fall down, as if the walls knew I was going. It was as if the house knew that I had left my mother behind praying to God. I felt very bad, but I also knew I had to do this.

I didn't know where we were going - I left it all to Azam. It was a long drive. After some time we stopped, and two more cars stopped behind us – his friends had been following us all the way. By the time we stopped to have something to eat I felt a little more relaxed. We were a long way from home now.

He told me that he was planning to take me back, but for now I should stay at a refuge. That was fine by me. All I wanted to do was collect my daughter.

He also said he had left his wife. I really didn't care what he wanted to do, as I was feeling sick and scared to death. We were now in Lahore, which is a huge city and one of the most beautiful cities in Pakistan. Here I knew no-one.

Finally we got to the airport. We stayed there the whole night. Azam went off to sleep, but I was much too scared and worried to sleep. I kept looking around, thinking my parents would appear at any moment. I asked one of the cleaners if there was a place to pray, and said some prayers.

In the morning they announced that the flight we were to catch was delayed for a few hours. By now I was so tired that I had no strength to walk around. At one point we got into an argument with a man who was looking at me. I had to beg Azam to let him off, as he was ready to punch him. I didn't want us to attract any attention.

At last we got on to the plane and took off. I sat there looking at the sky – I couldn't see much. Every time I thought of my family my heart missed a beat. I wondered what they were going through. I kept crying and then wiping the tears from my face.

First we were flying to Syria. There we had to wait 15 hours for the flight to England. Syria seemed to be a lovely country with lots of water. The people wore long Islamic robes and looked very high class.

As we waited, Azam's phone rang and he answered it. He looked puzzled when he heard the voice at the other end. "Hi" he said. "Yes I'm fine. How about you and the children?" It was his wife. He talked to her for a while, telling her he was with his friends in a restaurant. I heard her say "I love you" and he replied

"Me too, I'll see you soon".

My head was spinning. He started to say he was sorry but he had had to take the call and talk to her nicely. I told him it was OK, but of course it could not be OK.

I watched him as he sorted out all the stuff in his bags. I noticed a pair of silver high-heeled sandals and a pretty dress. I felt happy that he had bought me some gifts, as he didn't have to prove he cared for me. I picked them up.

"No, they're not yours" he said. I could see they were not my size.

"So who are they for?"

"My wife."

"What about the other things?"

"She told me to get all these things. I hope she likes them. What do you think?"

I went quiet and gave him a look.

"I don't like them" I said.

"Well she would like them, what's up with you?"

"I thought you said you had nothing to do with her?"

I didn't care that much. I just wanted to get home. But I did feel angry that he had lied to me again.

"What about you?" he said.

"What about me?"

"How could you get married like that, I'm ashamed of you!" he said.

I was in no position to say anything, so I just listened to what he had to say.

"You're lucky I'm still accepting you," he said. "Who would want a woman who has been married three times?"

I wanted to scream, but I could sense people were looking at us. I felt that if I did scream, every member of my family in both Pakistan and England would hear me. But he didn't stop.

"If you ask any man here if they would get married to a woman who has been married three times, they would say, of course not! Do you want me to ask?"

I thought to myself, well, why did you come and get me then?

He wandered off for a while and I sat there thinking. I was definitely going to collect my daughter and make my own way. I didn't need him or anyone else in my life. I had been through a lot and didn't want to spoil anyone else's life or have anyone else spoil mine. Once again I was being shoved to the ground, made to feel like a piece of rubbish.

Finally our flight was announced and we made our way to the departure lounge. Now we were only a few hours from home. The plan was to get help from the police, collect my daughter from my father's house and make my way to a refuge. We would have to see what happened after that.

We got our luggage and made our way to the arrivals. The plan was that as soon as we got to England he would take me to a rescue centre. His brother would collect us on the other side.

When the plane landed I walked out feeling free and breathing better than I had for years. I was home, back in my own world, a free woman. Now it would be just me, my daughter and Azam. He had helped me through all this, even though he was the biggest liar on earth.

Waiting to see me were all my family in the UK - my brothers, my cousins, my uncles. Perhaps I was special to them after all for them to come and welcome me like this! I walked towards the uncle who had arranged my last marriage and everyone just gathered around me. I looked on the other side, and there was Azam with his family - they were all there to receive him too.

Wherever I looked I saw faces I had known for years. They asked me why I had run away. I just cried. I was too ashamed of myself to say anything. I had always respected my elders. They kept asking me if I was going to make a fuss, and I said no.

CHAPTER 8

I can't remember too much of what happened after I arrived in England. I do know they took me to the house of one of my uncles and I was told to stay there. The next day I wanted to see my daughter, but she was at her grandmother's house and I didn't want her to know anything about how I had got back to England.

My brothers and sisters said I should make a visit to Pakistan as my mother had been so shocked by what I had done that she had had to be taken to hospital. They said she had had a minor heart attack. I couldn't stop crying with guilt and worry, and my sister cried with me.

They said we all had to go to see my mother as soon as possible. They were angry with me for putting my parents through so much. But they all said I had a lot of guts, and they sympathised that I had once again had to marry to meet my parents' wishes. They said that what I had done was way out of control and that I had to go back and show my face to the people in Pakistan, as there were rumours that I had run away and my mother couldn't bear that, which was why she was in hospital. They all said I just had to go for a week, and they would arrange a divorce from Nazir.

The next day I was taken to my mother's house to see my daughter. I was allowed only in the living room. My sister brought Henna in and we both got emotional seeing each other.

We hugged each other and she looked as sweet as always. After we had chatted for a while I had to let her go off to school. I told her I was going back to Pakistan for a week. My younger brother was taking her to school and bringing her back every day - he was like a mother and father to her. I knew she was in good hands.

Then I was taken back to my sister's house. I got so confused with how many days went by that looking back I think maybe I was given some drugs. I do remember that they took me to Tesco's to have some passport pictures taken and they made me sit in the middle of the back seat in case I escaped!

When we went inside everyone had their pictures taken in the booth. They all looked frightened. My sister walked with me step by step and I would laugh and tell her I wasn't going to run away.

I was told that as soon as we arrived in Pakistan we would go to see my mother in hospital. When we got into the cars to go to the airport I asked about my daughter, and my sister told me she was meeting me at the airport to see me off. I asked her to show me the tickets. She showed them to me. They were for a return flight the following week, so I knew I just had to suffer one more week of my family and then it would be back to normal life in England with me and my daughter.

When we reached the airport my daughter, my father's older sister, my uncles and my brother-in-law were already there. I sat next to my daughter and asked her about school. She was shy and we didn't say much. I kept telling her, I'll be back next week.

We all sat together as a big family and hot drinks were passed round. My aunt passed me some money and told me to give it to my daughter, and I gave it to her. My aunt was in tears, and I got emotional as well and hugged Henna tightly.

When it was time to leave and I walked through to the plane with my family, I looked back and saw my daughter standing there crying and holding some chocolates in her hands. I waved until I could see her no more. One of my cousins who was standing with her gave me a strange, deep look. I couldn't forget the look he gave me or that last wave to my daughter.

As we were checked on to the plane my sister held tightly on to me. I kept telling them I wasn't going away for long, but she wouldn't let go.

As we walked through the tunnel that led to the plane, the security people called to us to stop and then they called me over. My sister had to let go of me to let me walk towards the security men. I looked back at my family and my brother Shan's face seemed to have gone small and pale. My sisters' faces were pale too, as if they had lost a battle. I smiled and told them not to worry.

They searched me and went through my bag but found nothing and let me go. My family all looked very relieved as I walked back to them.

The flight to Pakistan took eight hours. All the time we were in the air Shan kept going to the back. I kept asking what he was doing – I thought he was chatting up the girls or something - but he was married and was a good boy, so I didn't think it was that.

Back in Pakistan we were met by a big car which had been sent by my father. Shan was still staying back - they told me he was waiting for someone. When all the luggage had been put in the car he took me on one side and told me my uncle had joined us.

"Which uncle?" I said. I had many.

"Uncle Saf" he said. Saf was my father's younger brother. He was a gangster, and everyone knew it. But I didn't care. I smiled and said, "Why is he hiding? I don't mind him being here." My brother waved and out came Saf – tall, skinny and handsome. He asked how I was, and then we all got into the car.

We chatted normally on the drive to the hospital, but every time I thought of my father my heart missed a beat. I was very scared and frightened, but I kept laughing to try to show them all I was fine.

My mother was lying on the bed with a drip beside her. My sisters hugged her and cried and I said hello, but she didn't respond. It was always like this, my sisters hugging their mother and me left to one side. I sat on a chair in the corner. I was crying too, but no one seemed to notice.

Then my father walked into the room. He did not look at me. My sisters ran to him and hugged him as if they would never let go, but I just sat there looking at the floor. This was nothing new to me either. My brother asked if I was OK and I told him I was fine, but he could see that I was not. I was shivering.

When we got to the house my mother-in-law and her sister were preparing food for us. They didn't speak to me either. I had told them I didn't want to see my husband - I just wanted to do my bit in Pakistan and then leave. It was only a week I had to spend with them.

My mother came home later that day. She had got better very quickly. When people came to see her they found me living there too and they could see I was still part of the family, just as they had wanted. When there were no visitors I spent hours sitting alone in my room by myself. I wasn't one of them any more. They were all precious, righteous people, but I was the evil one who had harmed everyone, so I had to sit alone.

The only thing that made me want to go on living was my daughter. I always thought of her. I had stopped thinking about Azam.

The days went past, and then the night we were to come back we heard that a young man we knew had killed himself by cutting his throat. The house went quiet, because everyone had left to visit his mother.

As I was sitting in my room I suddenly saw myself in the mirror. For some reason I felt terrified at seeing my own face. My sisters asked what was wrong, but when I told them I had been scared at the sight of my face in the mirror they roared with laughter. I pleaded with them not to laugh, but then I started laughing too. It was a long time since I had felt like laughing about anything.

A little later I went to pray. I was praying to God to help me get through my life when my sister came into my room and told me my father was asking for me. I felt terrified all over again. I was leaving the next day, so maybe they wanted to say something before I left. What would it be?

I walked from the hallway to my father's room. This was the first time I had been face to face with my father since my arrival. Everyone was there - my brother Shan, my sisters, my mother and uncles, everyone who had come with me. I was told to sit on a chair.

Then my uncle spoke. "You're not going back," he said. "You played a game with us. Who do you think we are?"

He started to say what a bitch I was. My mind was spinning. I couldn't take in what he was saying. I started to sob.

Then they wanted me to hear what my family had to say about me in England. My brother-in-law came on the phone and they put the speaker volume up so I could hear what he was saying. He told me I was a whore, a bitch, a slut. He said they all wanted me to be killed, because I was a shame on the family.

My own family, the family I had loved since I had been a child, wanted me to be killed! I feared death at that moment. God was never going to let me off, because I was so evil. I would go to hell.

Then my brother-in-law told me how they had decided to kill me. I would be taken to the river at night and thrown in. Accidents can happen in the dark, he said. I had always been terrified of water. I didn't want to die in the river in the dark. But no-one argued with him, no-one tried to stop him saying this. Even my mother just sat there, showing no trace of sympathy for her daughter.

"You lot can take it from here" said my brother-in-law. Then he rang off.

Then father took a gun from under his pillow. I stood up in shock, and he pointed at me. He pulled the trigger, but there was no bang, just a click. The gun must have been unloaded, but I nearly collapsed in fear. One of my sisters told me to run, but I couldn't. I just walked into the hallway, trembling so much I could hardly stand. There were so many doors in the hall and I didn't know which one to run to.

My father's uncle tried to grab the gun from my father. "Get away!" he shouted to me. I ran to my bedroom and then into my bathroom and locked the door.

I could hear my father banging on the door and his uncle trying to stop him. I banged my head against the wall and screamed and cried. I heard my sister shout "No Shani, stop!"

Then the bathroom door came down with a crash. My uncle was still struggling with my father. In the end he managed to push him away and get the gun from him. My uncle was a big strong man.

My uncle started to shout at me and say that all this trouble was my doing. I sat there feeling that perhaps I would not be killed just yet. I didn't think my uncle was going to let my father kill me.

Then my father's younger brother and my older brother Shan started banging on the door. My uncle opened the door and pushed his brother out of the room, and then he attacked me all over again. What a whore I was, what a bitch! My uncle kept saying to Shan, go on then, sort her out, but Shan wouldn't hit me, he just shouted at me.

At least Shan was not prepared to attack me. That gave me some strength.

After a while the kicking and beating stopped and they just stood there shouting insults at me down on the floor. It went on like this for what seemed like hours.

Finally my father walked in with Nazir. He asked Nazir what he wanted them to do with me. As my husband, he had first say.

"I want to keep her and I want her back in my life" Nazir said in a quiet voice.

"Take her then!" said my father.

They all left the room and I sat there with my husband. It was quiet at last. I heard the Azaan outside, the Islamic call to prayer, and realised it must be early morning.

Then my sister Sheana walked in. She came up to me and started taking my jewellery off me, all of it, piece by piece.

"Father wants everything back that he has given you," she said. I could hear my father shouting. "Get everything off her!" he said. "I want every single thing of hers out of my house!"

They opened my drawers, took everything out and put it into bags. They went through my purse and money cards and my sister even took the photo I kept of my daughter. In came Rehanna too, and she spat on my face and called me a whore and a bitch.

They had every right to do what they wanted, she said. They had given me so much but I had asked for a better future for me and my daughter, and that was too much for them. But at least it did not look as if they were going to throw me in the river.

Rehanna left and I wiped my face clean. My cousin walked in with a tray of breakfast, but I couldn't eat anything. Shan came to the door and looked at me. He nodded his head as if saying goodbye. That gave me a little hope.

Nazir made me stand up and led me to the hall. I could hardly walk. I was told I was being taken to my father's uncle's house. Sheana gave me my bag and my purse and I asked for my daughter's picture, and she went away and got it for me.

My father's uncle told me to go and say sorry to everyone. I didn't want to do that because it didn't seem right. They had all betrayed me and lied to me and called me a whore and a bitch. They had even talked about killing me. But of course I had no choice, I had to go in and see them.

I walked into my father's room and there they were all gathered together. My mother was sitting on the chair beside my father and my sisters were standing beside them, all looking as if they thought they were such good, fine people.

I mumbled that I was sorry, and no-one said anything. They told me to go, and I walked out of the house to the car that was waiting. My uncle and my brother were sitting on the lawn.

When I got to my father's uncle's house they led me to a bedroom and told me to stay there. No-one spoke to me and I didn't want to speak to them. Nazir tried to talk to me, but I had no strength to talk, not yet. I told him to leave me alone, and he slapped me and walked out of the door. I didn't feel it.

I lay on my bed all day. I couldn't eat anything and I didn't see anyone. There was no clock, but there was a little window in the roof and I could tell when it was evening because the sky was going dark outside.

Then I heard a car horn and the doorbell rang, and I knew the car had come to take my sister to the airport. I waited for them to come in to say goodbye, but they didn't appear. I hoped my husband would come so that I could beg him to let me say goodbye to my sisters, but finally I heard the gate shut and the car drive off. I got up and went to the door, but it was locked.

I sat on the floor and wept. How could they leave the country without me?

Nazir came in and saw me on the floor crying. I asked him if they had left a message for me but he said they had not.

"Maybe they wanted to see me but they weren't allowed to" I said. He said no, they had not wanted to see me. I screamed, and he slammed the door and left.

I got up and climbed back into bed, hoping perhaps that my sisters would still come back and say goodbye to me, but they did not. I felt scared that I might never see them again, never see my daughter again, and never see my home in England again.

They had left their baby sister to rot in hell. At that moment I wished my father had pulled the trigger.

EPILOGUE

Shahnaz was kept imprisoned in her family's home in Pakistan for 18 months, during which time she saw her daughter only on occasional visits from England. While she was there, Azam, back in England, reported the case to the British High Commission, who searched the family home on suspicion that she had been murdered. They attempted to interview Shahnaz in Pakistan, but on each occasion she was allowed to speak to them only via an intercom, with her family present to ensure she gave nothing away about their treatment of her.

Finally her third husband, Nazir, hoping to move to the UK to work, took Shahnaz to see the High Commission in Pakistan to reassure them that she was safe, in return for a promise that she would not incriminate the family. In 2005 she was finally allowed to return to Britain, where Nazir joined her the following year. They stayed with her family for a time before setting up home together.

Although Azam wrote to Shahnaz pleading with her to resume their relationship, she refused and has not seen him since.

Soon after returning to England, Shahnaz took up voluntary work at a local school. After studying social care and passing her exams, she has now become a qualified social worker specialising in child protection. Shahnaz, Nazir and Henna now live peacefully together.

Shahnaz' family now recognise that they made mistakes in trying to control her life choices, and she is once again on good terms with her father. None of her nephews or nieces have since been forced into arranged marriages.

Made in the USA
Middletown, DE
14 March 2022

62638162R00057